REGU

THE EXERCISE OF RIFLEMEN
AND
LIGHT INFANTRY
AND
INSTRUCTIONS FOR THEIR CONDUCT
IN
THE FIELD

PRINTED FOR THE WAR OFFICE

1814

The Naval & Military Press Ltd

published in association with

FIREPOWER
The Royal Artillery Museum
Woolwich

Published by
The Naval & Military Press Ltd
Unit 10 Ridgewood Industrial Park,
Uckfield, East Sussex,
TN22 5QE England
Tel: +44 (0) 1825 749494
Fax: +44 (0) 1825 765701
www.naval-military-press.com

in association with

FIREPOWER
The Royal Artillery Museum, Woolwich
www.firepower.org.uk

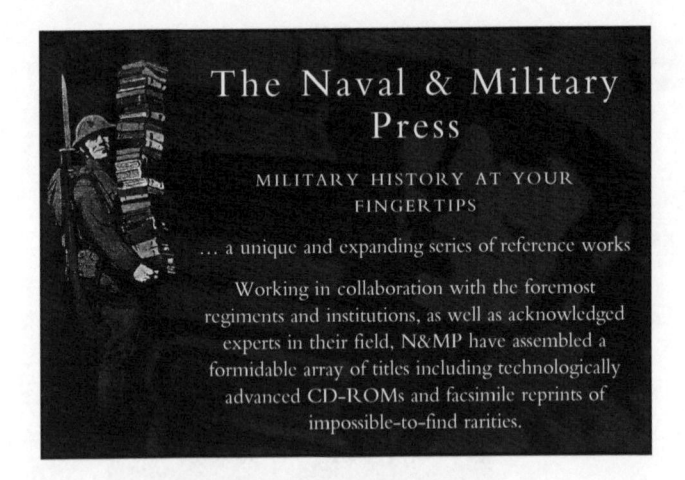

The Naval & Military Press

MILITARY HISTORY AT YOUR
FINGERTIPS

... a unique and expanding series of reference works

Working in collaboration with the foremost
regiments and institutions, as well as acknowledged
experts in their field, N&MP have assembled a
formidable array of titles including technologically
advanced CD-ROMs and facsimile reprints of
impossible-to-find rarities.

In reprinting in facsimile from the original, any imperfections are inevitably reproduced and the quality may fall short of modern type and cartographic standards.

Printed and bound by Antony Rowe Ltd, Eastbourne

HORSE GUARDS,
1st August, 1798.

THE original of the following Work, written by a German Officer of distinction, and much military experience, has been perused by HIS ROYAL HIGHNESS the COMMANDER-IN-CHIEF, and found to contain many excellent rules and observations, adapted to the usual modes of carrying on active service in the field, and much useful instruction to young officers, not familiarized by practice to the arduous duties to be performed in the face of an enterprising enemy: HIS ROYAL HIGHNESS has therefore been pleased to give directions for its being translated into English, in order that the officers of the army at large, and particularly those who may not have had the advantage of much personal experience in the field, may, by a studious attention to the various examples therein stated,

and

and to the useful lessons given for their conduct, imbibe that degree of military skill and information, which will enable them to discharge their duty to the satisfaction of their superiors, and their own honour, on the most trying occasions.

WILLIAM FAWCET,

Adjutant-General.

REGULATIONS

FOR

THE EXERCISE OF RIFLEMEN,

&c. &c.

PART I.

OF THE EXERCISE.

WHEN a company or battalion of riflemen is to act with closed ranks and files, the same regulations which are given to infantry in general, serve for them. And before the soldier is instructed in the manœuvres of light troops, he must be taught how to hold himself, to march, face, wheel, &c. as in regular infantry.

CHAP. I.

Of the Manual Exercise for the Rifle.

§ 1.

Of carrying the rifle
THE rifle is to be carried in the right hand, at arm's length, as in advanced arms, the cock resting upon the little finger, the thumb upon the guard, and fore finger under it, the upper part of the barrel close in the hollow of the shoulder, and the butt pressing upon the thigh.

§ 2.

The manual exercise.
TO PRESENT ARMS.

Attention.

At this word the flugelman steps six or more paces to the front.

Present

Present Arms. (Three motions.)

1st. The rifle is to be raised about two inches by the right hand, and brought forward a little from the shoulder, at the same time the left hand is brought briskly across the body, and seizes the rifle with a full grasp even with the shoulder.

2d. The right hand brings the rifle even with the face, and opposite the left eye, grasps the small of the stock, turning the lock outwards, the left hand seizes it by the stock, so that the little finger touches the hammer spring, on a level with the chin, the left elbow close to the butt.

3d. The rifle is brought in a straight line to the *present*, the lock turned inwards, and even with the bottom of the waistcoat, the right foot is placed about three inches behind the left heel, the right hand holding the small of the stock between the fore finger and thumb, the knuckles upwards, the three other fingers shut in the hand.

Shoulder Arms. (Two motions.)

1st. The rifle is brought quickly across the body to the right side, the right hand slipping round into the original position when shouldered, the left quits its hold, and seizes the rifle again smartly even with

the

the right shoulder, at the same time the right foot is brought up in a line with the left.

2*d*. The left hand quits the rifle, and is brought as quickly as possible flat upon the left thigh.

Order Arms.

At the word *arms*, the left hand seizes the rifle even with the right shoulder, the rifle, as in the first motion of the *present*, is raised about two inches, the right hand quits its hold, grasps the rifle round the muzzle, and brings it gently to the ground, even with the toe of the right foot, the wrist pressing against the side and elbow as close as possible. The left hand is brought as before on the left thigh.

Shoulder Arms.

At the word *arms*, the rifle is thrown at once into the right shoulder by a jerk of the right hand; the left catches it till the right seizes the rifle in the proper place, and is then instantly brought to its original position on the left thigh: but this must be done with the quickness of one motion.

In the performance of this, as indeed of every other motion, the greatest care is to be taken to prevent the rifle falling to the ground, as it is an arm easily damaged, and in the field, where time and
opportunity

opportunity cannot always be found to repair it, the service of a rifleman is lost by every such instance of inattention.

Support Arms.

The rifle is brought across the body with the guard upwards, by bending the right arm, the left hand is laid across the right.

Carry Arms.

The rifle is brought smartly on the right side, and the left hand on the left thigh.

Trail Arms.

The left hand seizes the rifle at the second pipe, the right close over the sight, and trails it on the right side at arm's length, the left falls back on the left thigh.

Shoulder Arms.

The rifle is brought to the advance, as from the order.

FROM THE ORDER TO TRAIL ARMS.

Trail Arms.

The right hand seizes the rifle as low as possible without constraint, then raises and catches it just above the sight.

FROM THE TRAIL TO ORDER ARMS.

Order Arms.

The rifle slides gently through the right hand to the ground, when even with the right toe the right hand again grasps the muzzle.

CHAP.

CHAP. II.

Of Priming and Loading, and of Firing at the Target.

§ 1.

THE words of command for firing and loading are as follow: *Of priming and loading.*

1. *The Company will Prime and Load.*

2. *Attention.*

At which the flugelman steps in front.

3. *Prepare to Load.*

For which the flugelman gives the time in two motions.

1*st*. Is the same as the first motion, in the *present*.

2*d*. The soldier half faces to the right, and in the motion brings down the rifle to an horizontal position just above the right hip, the left hand supports it at the swell of the stock, the elbow resting against the side, the right thumb against the hammer, the knuckles upwards, and elbow pressing against the butt, the lock inclining a little to the body to prevent

vent the powder from falling out. The officer now warns the men in going through the loading motions.

To wait for the Words of Command.

At which caution the flugelman falls in.

At the word, *One,*

The pan is pushed open by the right thumb, the right hand then seizes the cartridge with the three first fingers.

Two,

The cartridge is brought to the mouth, and placed between the two first right double teeth, the end twisted off and brought close to the pan.

Three,

The priming is shaken into the pan; in doing which, to see that the powder is properly lodged, the head must be bent; the pan is shut by the third and little finger, the right hand then slides behind the cock, and holds the small part of the stock between the third and little finger and ball of the hand.

Four,

The soldier half faces to the left; the rifle is
brought

brought to the ground with the barrel outwards, by sliding it with care through the left hand, which then seizes it near the muzzle, the thumb stretched along the stock, the butt is placed between the heels, the barrel between the knees, which must be bent for that purpose ; the cartridge is put into the barrel, and the ramrod seized with the fore finger and thumb of the right hand.

Rod,

The ramrod is drawn quite out by the right hand, the left quits the rifle and grasps the ramrod the breadth of a hand from the bottom, which is sunk one inch into the barrel.

Home,

The cartridge will be forced down with both hands, the left then seizes the rifle about six inches from the muzzle, the soldier stands upright again, draws out the ramrod with the right hand, and puts the end into the pipe.

Return,

The ramrod will be returned by the right hand, which then seizes the rifle below the left.

Shoulder.

Shoulder.

The right hand brings the rifle to the right shoulder; turning the guard outwards, the left seizes it above the hammer-spring till the right has its proper hold round the small of the stock, when the left is drawn quickly to the left thigh.

When the recruits are sufficiently perfect in firing by these distinct and separate words of command, they should be accustomed to go through the motions with the following words of command only:

1. *The Company will Prime and Load.*

2. *Attention.*

At which the flugelman steps in front.

3. *Prepare to Load.*

To this motion the flugelman gives the time.

4. *Load.*

The flugelman falls in. Every motion in loading, as described above, is to be performed; and here officers are required to pay particular attention, that no single motion be omitted, as it is of more consequence

consequence that a rifle should be properly, than expeditiously, loaded.

---

§ 2.

RIFLEMEN must at first be accustomed to make ready and present, methodically; and in this they should be thoroughly practised, for they will seldom be in a situation to fire by word of command.

Of making ready and presenting

The firings may be divided under three heads: viz. *in advancing, in retreating,* and *on the spot.*

The method of firing in advancing and retreating by signal, will be explained in the following sections.

To fire on the spot with closed ranks, the following words of command will be given:

1. *The Company will Fire.*

2. *Company.*

At this word, the right hand file of each platoon takes three quick paces to the front, the rear rank man steps to the right of his file leader.

3. *Ready.*

3. *Ready.*

At this word, the rifle is brought by the right hand before the centre of the body, the left seizes it, so that the little finger rests upon the hammer-spring, and the thumb stretched along the stock, raising it to the height of the mouth, the right thumb on the cock, and four fingers under the guard; when cocked, which must be done gently, the right hand grasps the small of the stock.

4. *Present.*

The soldier half faces to the right, the butt is placed in the hollow of the right shoulder, the right foot steps back about eighteen inches behind the left, the left knee is bent, the body brought well forward, the left hand, without having quitted its hold, supports the rifle close before the lock, the right elbow raised even with the shoulder, the fore finger on the trigger, the head bent, and cheek resting on that of the rifle, the left eye shut, the right taking aim through the sight: as soon as the rifleman has fixed upon his object, he fires without waiting for any command. When he has fired, the right hand quits its hold in facing to the right about, the left swings the rifle round into an horizontal position with the barrel downwards; the rifleman resumes his post in the platoon, in fronting to the left about,

about, brings his rifle into the position to prime and load, half cocks, and proceeds to load, going through the motions as above without further words of command.

As soon as the riflemen are perfect in this, they will be instructed, that at the signal of the horn to *commence firing*, the two right hand files of each platoon or section, according as the company may be told off, are immediately to take three paces to the front, the rear rank men step to the right of their file leaders, present, and each fires as he gets a proper aim, then resumes his place in the company as above mentioned, and loads again: when the two first files have fired the two next advance, and so on through the company.

This mode of firing is necessary to prevent the whole from being unloaded at the same time; when the company therefore has fired once according to the above regulations, every file on being loaded again will advance three paces, and each man will take his aim and fire, and then immediately resume his place in the company, load, &c. When it is required that the firing should cease, the signal to *cease firing* will be made by the bugle, after which not a shot must be heard. The officers, who must invariably remain in the line during this firing, are on no account to stir from the spot; and when the signal to *cease firing* is made, and every man loaded and shouldered, they will dress their platoons. Too much attention cannot be given to the above rule, for the preservation of the alignment will entirely depend upon a strict observance of it.

§ 3.

Of firing at the target.

THE above regulations for firing with cartridges will only be applicable when a corps of riflemen is required to act in close order, an instance which will very seldom occur, provided this arm is put to its proper use, and officers will observe in all cases, where riflemen act as such, and whenever it is practicable, their men are to load with the powder measure and loose ball; the principal instructions therefore for recruits, will be how to load with the loose ball, and to fire at the target; the loading with cartridge is a secondary object. To this end, the rifle recruit must from the first, in addition to his other exercise, be constantly practised in firing at the target.

In firing at a mark, it is to be observed, that the target should be at least five feet in diameter; for if it were smaller, the unpractised recruit would be apt to miss so often as to despair of hitting it; and to become expert, a man should find encouragement, and even amusement, in this practice. Another disadvantage in its being too small would be, that the rifleman

rifleman could not become acquainted with his rifle, as, in missing the target altogether, he could not ascertain whether he had shot too much to the right, or too much to the left; whereas a target of a proper size, and painted in circles, being easily hit, the rifleman sees at once the fault he has made, and learns to correct it. The rifle recruit must at first be taught to fire at the target without a rest, for if he accustoms himself to make use of a support, he will rarely fire true without one; but as this method will at first be found difficult, and only rendered easy by practice, he should begin by firing at the distance of fifty yards, and increase it by degrees to three hundred.

The rifleman must be made acquainted with the nature of the sights and aim of the rifle; he must be taught to use the plaster, (i.e. a piece of greased leather or rag) in loading with a loose ball, and how to force it down the barrel, observing that it should lie close upon the powder, without being driven with a degree of force which might bruise the grains: after every shot which strikes the target, the rifleman must observe whether he pointed too high or too low, or too much to the right or left, and correct himself accordingly. The officers will take care that, during this practice, every man learns the proper charge for his rifle, and if any rifle should be found faulty, it is to be remarked that the necessary alterations may be made. Riflemen must also be practised to fire and load as they lie on the ground.

CHAP.

CHAP. III

Of Extending and Closing again.

§ 2.

To extend, from the right, left, or centre. Fig. I. When the company is formed at close order, and is required to extend from the right, the words of command will be given as follow:

To the Left extend.

At this word of command the company, except the right hand file, faces to the left, moves on in quick time, casting the eyes over the right shoulder, so that each file when at two paces distant from his right hand file may halt, front, and dress by the right. The rear rank steps to the right, in order, if necessary, to march or fire without impediment through the intervals of the front rank. This is the usual distance between files, at which light troops when ordered to extend will form; but in particular cases, when they are required to cover the front of a corps, or mask a manœuvre, the commanding officer will signify at what distance the files are to form from each other, before he gives the order for them to extend themselves.

When

When the company is to extend from the left, the word of command will be given. Fig. II.

To the Right extend.

The whole, except the left hand file, face to the right, in taking their distance look over the left shoulder, halt, front, and dress by the left. The rear rank, as in opening to the left, take ground to the right of their file leaders.

When to extend from the centre, the word of command will be given. Fig. III.

From the Centre extend.

At which the right wing faces and moves to the right, as in extending from the left; the left wing performs the same movements as when extending from the right; the centre file stands fast.

As soon as the recruits are perfect in this mode of extending, the words of command of *from right, left,* or *centre extend,* are laid aside, and the commanding officer takes post on the wing, or point from which the company is to extend; and orders the bugle to sound the signal to extend; and should the distance proposed to be taken between the files be more than two paces (the usual extended order), he will signify, before the signal to extend is made, at what distance the defiles are to form, at 3, 4, 5, or 6 paces.

On the signal to extend, the files open from the spot where the commanding officer has placed himself with the bugle. When extended, the riflemen trail their arms. If detached corps should happen to be without a bugle, the officer must make use of the before-mentioned words of command to extend.

Of Closing again.

When an extended corps is to close again

On the signal from the bugle *to close,* every man faces and closes briskly to the point from whence the signal is given; the whole shoulder their rifles and dress; in this movement the files must be careful not to intermix, to prevent the confusion that would unavoidably arise from their doing so. Should the commanding officer have no bugle with him to give the signal, he must give the word of command *Close.*

CHAP.

CHAP. IV.

Of Firing in extended Order, and of Skirmishing.

§ 1.

WHEN riflemen or light corps are to fire *from the spot* in extended order, the bayonets of the latter must be first unfixed, the commandieg officer then orders the horner to give the signal to commence firing. At this signal the front rank makes ready, presents (each man selecting his particular object), and fires: as soon as the rear rank man sees his file leader put the ball into his piece, he makes ready, and fires through the intervals of the front rank; and when the rear rank men have got their balls into their pieces, each man gives notice to his file leader to fire. In this manner the fire is continued *on the spot*, till the signal is given to cease firing.

Of firing on the spot.

§ 2.

Of firing in advancing.

In firing in advancing, the commanding officer first orders the signal to *march* to be sounded, and immediately after the signal to *fire*.

On this the rear rank moves briskly six paces before the front rank, each man having passed to the right of his file leader, makes ready, takes his aim, and fires; and as soon as he has loaded again, trails his rifle. When the serjeant of the front rank sees the rear rank has fired, he steps in front, gives a signal with his whistle, upon which the front rank moves briskly six paces before the rear rank, each man then presents, takes aim, and fires; following the directions that have been given to the rear rank. Thus each rank continues advancing and firing alternately. If the firing in advancing is to cease, the commanding officer orders the signal for halt, after which not a shot must be heard.

§ 3.

Of firing in retreating.

At the signal of the bugle to *commence firing*, immediately followed by the signal to *retreat*, the first rank (namely, that which happens to be in front) makes

makes ready, takes aim, and fires, goes to the right about, marches with a quick step twelve paces in the rear of the second rank, fronts and loads. As soon as the serjeant on the flank of the second rank sees that the first is formed and loading, he steps two paces to the front, and gives the signal with his whistle, upon which the second rank makes ready, takes aim, and fires; then faces to the right about, marches with a quick step twelve paces into the rear of the first, fronts and loads. In this manner both ranks retire, supporting each other. When the fire in retiring is to cease, the commanding officer orders the signal for *halt* to be made.

§ 4.

THE companies being sufficiently instructed in the Of skir-
above firings, they will proceed to the practice of mishing, Fig. VI.VII
them, in which one general principle must be observed; namely, that never more than one half of a body of riflemen must be sent forward to skirmish, the other half remain formed and ready to support. If a battalion or company of riflemen is to make an attack, or by means of the above disposition keep the enemy at a distance from their front, the commanding officer will first signify, whether the right

or

or left platoons are to advance. If the latter, the left platoon of each company moves briskly fifty paces forwards, the right half of that platoon then *halts* with closed ranks, the left half moves sixty paces further to the front and extends its files, so as to cover completely the front of the main body from which it is detached. Whenever right platoons advance to skirmish, right half platoons must be pushed on in their front and extend themselves to the left, and *vice versâ*.

If the signal is sounded to *march*, the platoons which remain formed in line, and the half platoons which were advanced fifty paces in front of them, move forward in ordinary time, taking care to preserve their intervals. The skirmishers who have been pushed on in front, conduct themselves in the same manner as in firing in advancing. If the signal for *halt* is given, the whole corps halts, and the skirmishers cease firing; but keep their ground: on the signal for *retreat*, the whole corps, except the skirmishers, face to the right about, and retire in ordinary time, paying the greatest attention to the preservation of distances. The platoons which have been pushed on in front in extended order, conduct themselves in the same manner as in firing in retreating. On the signal to *halt*, the whole halts, fronts, and the skirmishers cease firing.

At the signal to *close*, the half platoons which have extended themselves in front to skirmish, fall back on the half which has remained formed in their
rear.

rear. At the second signal to *close*, the advanced platoons retreat in quick time, and take their places in the line.

When a company or battalion has been formed for an attack in the above manner, and the signal for *alarm* is sounded, the skirmishers retire with the greatest celerity through their respective intervals in the battalion; in the rear of which they form and resume their several stations in the line.

This manœuvre will be requisite only when the battalion is to attack, or may have occasion to make use of its whole fire: the skirmishers therefore will not wait for another, but will retire as fast as they can through the intervals, as above; but the quarter platoons will remain formed, and move with a firm and quick step into their proper places. The officers of the detached platoons must direct their principal attention to combine in such a manner the movements of their half platoons and skirmishers, with those of the battalion or corps, as always to keep parallel with them, and to preserve the proper distances of the extended order they have been directed to take.

It may happen that an entire company be required to extend itself for the purpose of covering the front of a corps, without leaving any part formed as a reserve. In this case the company will trail arms, advance in close order, and when arrived at the proper distance, will extend itself with all possible celerity. If the company is detached from the right wing,

wing, it will extend to the left; if from the left wing, it will extend to right; and if from the centre, to both the flanks.

Fig. VIII. Should it be necessary to retire across a plain; on the battalion going to the right about, the right and left flank files of each platoon remain fronted; in retreating, the battalion will carefully preserve the intervals left by the above files, whose business it is to extend themselves to cover its retreat, following it at the distance of thirteen paces, and by their fire endeavouring to keep off the enemy's flankers: for this purpose, riflemen should be practised to load and fire in marching; during this manœuvre it will be particularly necessary to caution the flankers against expending their fire all at the same time.

If attacked by cavalry, the signal for *halt* will be first made, on which the battalion fronts; the signal for *retreat* will then be sounded, on which the skirmishers fall into their respective places in the line.

If the battalion is to continue its retreat, it will face to the right about; the skirmishing files remain fronted as before. When the retreat has been effected to the point proposed, the signal to *halt* is made, on which the battalion fronts, the skirmishers are called in, and the whole dresses by the centre.

CHAP.

CHAP. V.

Of the Formation of the Chain and Advanced Guard.

§ 1.

THE object of this branch of the duty of light troops is to scour a tract of country by means of numerous and detached bodies, clearing the woods and enclosures of the enemies posts, and in a word, to establish a complete chain of your own troops, by occupying, as far as circumstances will permit, every advantageous spot; taking particular care, however, that your own posts are so stationed as to have easy communication, and the power of mutually supporting each other. *[margin: Formation of the chain.]*

When a company of light infantry is destined to form the chain without any other corps to support it, the commanding officer signifies that one fourth of it, *i. e.* one half platoon or section, will remain formed as a reserve: suppose, for instance, the fourth section is fixed on for this service; in this case the three first advance fifty paces in quick time; the order is then given to *form the chain to the right or left*, or as circumstances may require; the signal from the bugle is immediately given, and *[margin: Fig. IX.]*

the detachment extends in divisions of two files at ten paces distant from each other; the fourth section remains formed. This disposition being made, the signal from the bugle is given to *march*. The chain moves forward in ordinary time, taking care to preserve the distance and alignement. The section of reserve follows at the distance of fifty paces, in order to give support to any part of the chain that may be attacked.

On the signal *halt*, the whole halts and dresses. If the chain is to fire, the signal is made to *commence firing;* on which the right flugelman of each division of the chain takes three paces to the front and fires, falls back into his place again and loads: the other three men perform the same singly; and by this means the fire is kept up, without intermission, till the signal is made to *cease firing*.

At the signal to *retreat*, the whole chain faces to the right about, and retreats in ordinary time. On the signal to *halt*, the whole chain halts and fronts. If it is to *incline to the left*, it faces to the left, and takes ground to the left; if to *incline to the right*, it faces and takes ground to the right; or the object of gaining ground on either flank may be obtained with equal facility by an oblique movement. On the signal to *close*, the whole chain closes to the point from whence the sound is given.

Fig. X.   Should the two flank platoons of a corps of light infantry be ordered to form the chain, or extend themselves (as circumstances may require), in order

by

by this means to mask the formation of the battalion, or to keep the enemy at a distance, in a country, where his front is difficult of approach; the two flank platoons will advance in quick time the distance which may be directed, and when arrived on the spot, the right flank platoon forms the chain to the left, and the left flank platoon to the right, proceeding according to the directions already given for extending, and for the formation of the chain. On the signal being made to *close*, the platoons close to the point from which they extended, and both resume their situations on the flanks of the corps as quickly as possible.

---

§ 2.

The company is told off into four half platoons, or sections. The commanding officer, with the first half platoon, marches in front of the corps to which he forms the advanced 'guard, in the day-time, five hundred paces, but in the night, or in hazy weather, three hundred only. The second section is detached two hundred paces in front of the first, and a party of a serjeant and six men is pushed on one hundred paces further, which forms the head of the advanced guard. The third and fourth half platoons are

Disposition of a company of riflemen or light infantry, which is to form an advanced guard.

placed

placed three hundred paces to the right and left of the first, and even with it, taking care to preserve, as much as possible, the above distance from it, and detaching one hundred paces forwards, and in an oblique direction to the outer flank, a non-commissioned officer and six men.

The duty of the advanced guard is to scour the whole country in its front, penetrating through woods and enclosures, and searching into villages. If the patroles meet with an enemy, the officer of the half platoons informs the captain of the company, who reports the same by a steady non-commissioned officer to the commanding officer of the corps.

The commanding officer of the advanced guard will of course have been previously directed, whether in case of falling in with an enemy, he is to attack or merely to amuse him with his skirmishers, or whether he is to fall back. In the last instance he must not retire with the main body, but, by withdrawing in an oblique direction, leave a clear stage for the operations of that corps against the enemy. He will by this movement avoid the possibility of confusion ensuing from the retreat of his own troops, which, under particular circumstances, may unavoidably become precipitate. On the signal to *march*, the whole advanced guard moves forward. On the signal *halt*, the whole halts, keeping, however, the disposition. If the signal to *close* is sounded, the non-commissioned officers' detachments join their respective half platoons; and on the

the second signal to *close*, the second, third, and fourth half platoons close and form to the first. When one single platoon is to compose an advanced guard, it will be told off in four sections, which are then to represent the four half platoons. In every other respect the regulations and directions given in the foregoing paragraph are applicable in the present instance.

PART II.

Of the Service of Light Troops in the Field.

During the campaign, light troops are usually cantoned in villages, and are not provided with camp equipage. They may, however, be occasionally required to occupy ground on the flank of a corps in the line of encampment; the men must, in that case, construct huts of earth, or boughs of trees, and will perform all the camp duties, and in every respect comply with the regulations laid down for the discipline of regular infantry.

CHAP. I.

§ 1.

Of Patroles in General.

Supposing a patrole to consist of a serjeant and twelve men, the serjeant detaches two men and a corporal in front, and two on each flank, the latter extending themselves to the right and left as far as possible, without losing sight of the main body; but the distance of these skirmishers, both in front and on

Disposition to be observed by a patrole in reconnoitring ground, villages or woods, or if defiles, hollow ways, or enclosures, are to be passed during the march.

on either flank, must be regulated by local circumstances; in an open and plain country, they may venture to extend themselves further from the main body than in one that is enclosed or hilly. On coming to an enclosure, one man advances into it and examines it closely; the other, remaining behind, keeps upon the watch, and takes care to be always ready to support his comrade, in case of his being attacked.

---

§ 2.

On arriving at an hill.

On coming to an hill, one man will ascend; the other, remaining at the bottom, will be given to understand, by a signal concerted between them, whether the enemy occupy any part of it or not. If an enemy is discovered, both the skirmishers must conceal themselves, and having ascertained as nearly as possible the strength of the enemy, one must endeavour to join the patrole, to give the intelligence; upon which the patrole should retire, and, if possible, throw itself into an ambuscade, to observe the enemy's motions. When a flanker sees a detachment of the enemy advancing immediately upon the patrole, and that he is not able *by any other means* to give the alarm of their approach, he must fire, which will be the signal for all the flankers to join the

the main body, or the signal will be given for assembly, and the patrole with united force will attack the enemy if equal to him in numbers, or will secure its retreat by a firm resistance, if the superior strength of the enemy makes it imprudent to risk an attack.

§ 3.

WHEN a patrole marches through an enclosed country, or one much intersected by hedges, the flankers must be sent on each side of them, in order to examine them thoroughly; in doing which, they must always keep as near as possible in a line with the main body, and resume their proper stations, as soon as they have passed any obstacle which may have drawn them out of their direction. It may sometimes be necessary for flankers to get to the tops of trees, for the purpose of reconnoitring, and on no account must they leave any high ground behind them, without first viewing the environs from it.

In passing hedges and enclosures.

§ 4.

IN marching over an open country, and where objects are seen at a great distance, it will not be

In traversing open ground.

necessary

necessary to send out skirmishers on the flanks, unless an house or an enclosure is perceived at a distance; in which case they must be detached to examine it thoroughly. By night, or in hazy weather, flankers are in all situations indispensably necessary, and must be particularly careful to regulate their movement by that of the main body.

§ 5.

In passing through an hollow way.

GREAT precaution is requisite when a patrole is under the necessity of passing an hollow way in order to guard against a surprise or being cut off. To avoid this, the patrole should be divided into files, which will follow each other at such a distance that each may be able to distinguish the two men immediately before them; by this arrangement, an enemy will only be able to perceive the two men in front, and the whole patrole will be alarmed, either by their comrades in front being attacked, or by their fire upon the enemy. If there should be turnings or windings in the hollow way, which prevent those in the rear from seeing the file in front of them, the latter must give notice of the presence of an enemy by firing a shot.

§ 6.

§ 6.

When a wood presents itself in front of the march, through which the patrole must pass, the flank skirmishers are sent to the skirts of it; they must, however, keep so much within the wood as not to be perceived from without; the main body marches directly through, but if possible by some other road than that which is commonly used. For the security of a patrole, when it is a strong one, detachments should be left at the entrance of the wood, to sustain the main body in its march through, and to give the alarm in case of the approach of an enemy. If the wood is of great extent, small patroles should be sent in front and on the flanks of the main body; and small intermediate patroles must be sent out, keeping at the distance of 4 or 500 yards from those in front of them, whose object will be to examine all cross roads, there being little apprehension for the safety of these detachments, supposing even the enemy to be in ambuscade in the wood. Three men will be sufficient for these patroles, two of which will advance in a line, and keep within sight of each other; the third following them and placing himself so as always to keep them both in view: by this means, should the most advanced patrole be carried off by the enemy, the second and following ones would escape, and the main body would have timely notice of the danger. In returning the patrole should

In marching through a wood.

take

take a different route from that by which it advanced, for the better chance of discovering the enemy; indeed, it must be considered as a general rule, that no patrole should return by the way it came; nor in case of being attacked, and obliged to retreat, should it ever fall back in a direct line upon the main body. Bye roads are always to be preferred to the main route, either in returning from the patroles or in retreating before an enemy; in patroling through a wood, care should be taken not to venture too far, and that the skirmishers are not at too great a distance from each other, for fear of hazy weather, or the approach of night.

―――

§ 7.

In marching through a defilé.

BEFORE a patrole ventures into a defilé, the two men advanced in front must examine it well, and at the same time flankers must reconnoitre the ground on the right and left of it, where it is probable the enemy might lie in ambuscade. In returning, a patrole should if possible avoid a defilé it has before passed. When the defilé has been passed, a few men may be left at the extremity of it, to give the alarm by a shot, in case a detachment of the enemy should attempt to cut off the patrole; these men will eventually

ally disconcert the enemy's plans, who may naturally conceive them to be the head of a detachment passing the defilé, as a support to the patrole.

§ 8.

When a patrole is to reconnoitre a village, the directions that have been already given for its conduct during the march must be strictly adhered to. Whether the patrole is a strong one or not, it must halt at a few hundred paces from the village, assemble all the skirmishers, and lie concealed; a few men must then be sent towards the village, and must endeavour to seize one of the inhabitants, and conduct him to the officer commanding the patrole, in order that he may be examined respecting the presence of the enemy. If upon diligent inquiry it is found that the enemy are in the village, the patrole must make its retreat: the deposition of one person should not, however, be depended upon; the men who have been sent to the village must endeavour if possible, to take another person, who must be separately examined, to see whether his report coincides with the former one. If after all inquiry it appears that the enemy are not in the village, some men must be sent into it, and small parties to the right and left

In reconnoitring a village.

left of it to examine its environs, and all the avenues must at the same time be occupied. The men who were sent into the village must immediately repair to the mayor or chief magistrate of the place, and make him accompany them to search all the houses, stables, barns, and all other places where the enemy might be concealed. If they find all safe, the men must return to the main body, and make their report. After this, should the commander of the patrole wish still to be himself convinced of the truth of the report, he may go in person into the village, accompanied by a few men, for prudence would suggest the impropriety of taking the whole patrole, as, notwithstanding the former search, it is still possible the enemy may be in ambuscade, and only watching the opportunity of the whole detachment being in the village, to attack it to advantage. When a non-commissioned officer commands a patrole, before he leaves a village he has been directed to examine, he should require a certificate of his having been there. When a patrole is to reconnoitre a village by night, the whole must assemble at some distance in front of it, as in patroling by day, and the environs must be examined ; but the men who are sent into the village must, in this instance, be directed to creep gently along the fronts of the houses, and particularly along those of the public houses, looking at the same time in at the windows, and endeavouring to distinguish whether any of the enemy are within. Should this be found impracticable, they must con-

ceal

ceal themselves, and wait the opportunity of some inhabitant passing, whom it will be their object to carry off to the commanding officer of the patrole with as little noise as possible, and without raising any alarm. If it should appear to be certain, from the report that the prisoner makes, and from other intelligence, that the enemy are not in the village, the same directions must be followed as have been already laid down for the day patrole; but should the enemy be in the village, the patrole must retire; an attempt, however, should be made to carry off one of his videttes, in order to gain more certain accounts. Whatever has been said with respect to villages, is applicable also to any place or town.

§ 9.

When skirmishers give notice of the approach of the enemy, the patrole should endeavour to conceal itself, the object of a patrole being to reconnoitre a country, and to get intelligence of the enemy, their movements, &c.; all engagement should be avoided, and, unless absolutely compelled to fight, a patrole should always endeavour to get away undiscovered. If a patrole allows itself to be unnecessarily drawn into an affair with one of the enemy's, it must run

On meeting an enemy.

an

an equal risk of being captured, and the service it was to have performed remains unaccomplished, so that the army of detachment, from whence the patrole was sent out, may wait in vain for the intelligence that was expected from it. If a patrole should be unavoidably engaged in an affair, the officer commanding it will send immediate notice by two trusty men to the corps from which he was detached, and at the same time a written report of whatever information he may have been able to obtain, which he should always have ready in case of such an event. When a patrole is to be sent out, every sort of instruction for its conduct during the march should be communicated to the men. The greatest attention in the officer commanding a patrole will be requisite to watch the conduct of his men: they must be attentive, obedient, and vigilant, from the moment of their departure till their return; and, under pain of the severest punishment, they must be forbidden to go into any public-house during the march; they should therefore be supplied with their complete ration of provisions. A patrole should always endeavour to conceal its march; therefore woods and enclosures are to be preferred in its progress through a country. Bridges should be avoided, for fear of ambuscades or of being cut off. If, however, a bridge must of necessity be passed, a few men should be posted at it, to give the alarm to the patrole on the approach of the enemy. In this case it will be advertised of the danger by a shot; by which
means

means it may gain time to repass the bridge, and at least avoid being cut off. Should every thing remain quiet, at the expiration of a certain time, previously determined, the men who were left at the bridge will follow, and join the patrole.

If the patrole is forced to pass places, where, notwithstanding every precaution, there is still a probability of being cut off, small posts must be left at such places, or the patrole should be divided into a number of small detachments, advance by different routes, and some place should be appointed for a rendezvous of the whole.

When a patrole finds itself *unexpectedly* in presence of an enemy, if of equal force it should attack: but should the enemy's numbers be very superior, and there remain no possibility of getting away undiscovered, the patrole must disperse, and each man save himself as he can. In such a case, and when, from an apprehension of danger, the patrole is advancing in small detachments, one in front of the other, as soon as those in the rear are made aware of the enemy being so superior, they must immediately retreat, without waiting for the detachments in their front. It is the duty of a commanding officer of a patrole to point out to each man all the dangers to be expected, the manner in which he is to conduct himself in retiring singly, the roads that are open to him in such a case, the places at which the patrole may rendezvous, and (should that be impracticable) the position of the detachment or army, to which he must endeavour to make his escape. The above instructions it is absolutely necessary to impress strongly on the minds of the men, in order that each man may know how he is to save himself under the above-mentioned events.

As the greatest prejudice may arise from a patrole having committed the most trifling error, and as, on the contrary, the greatest advantage may be derived to an army from the good conduct of one, all the above instructions, and as many more as may be thought useful, should be *explained to the men in the clearest terms* previous to the marching off, and during the march of the patrole.

CHAP.

CHAP. II.

Of the Advanced Guard, Flank Patroles, and Rear Guard, and of their several Duties on a March.

§ 1.

It is a rule which must always be attended to, that no column, regiment, or detachment, whether it be near, or at a distance from the enemy, marches without an advanced guard, and flank patroles, in order to reconnoitre the country, and prevent the possibility of an attack before the column has time to form, or to look for and dislodge the enemy when he is supposed to be in the neighbourhood, though no account is received of his exact position.

General rule.

§ 2.

The distribution of the advanced guard, and flank patroles, remains as has been before directed. The intention being, that they should be sent as far in front and on the flanks as possible, it becomes equally

Distribution of the advanced guard and flank patroles.

ly necessary, that they again should detach in their front and on their flanks (in as large proportion as their numbers will allow) skirmishers, whose business it will be to examine closely all objects which present themselves on the march, to traverse all enclosures, and the like. Skirmishers must always be in parties of two men each, so that while one is employed in examining any object, the other may remain on the look out, and if any thing approach, or is perceived at a distance, the one may immediately make a report to the body from which he is detached, while the other keeps his eye constantly on the object till the return of his comrade.

---

§ 3.

Of the distance of the advanced guard and flank patroles from the column

The distance at which an advanced guard and flank patroles should keep from the columns must be determined by local circumstances, and by the strength of the column. They should, however, be always at such a distance, that if they should be unexpectedly attacked, the column may have time to put itself in a posture of defence; and also, that if defilés, villages, or woods, present themselves on the line of march, they may be examined thoroughly before the arrival of the head of the column, that there

there may then be no delay. The skirmishers must be very cautious during the march, not to be cut off from the advanced guard; and the same precautions are necessary for the advanced guard, with respect to the column.

§ 4.

SKIRMISHERS, whether from the flank patroles or advanced guard, are to stop every person they meet, to question them respecting the enemy, and then conduct them to the main body, where they will be detained or released according to circumstances. Persons so taken may be occasionally found useful as guides for the bye roads, or to point out such places as might serve as ambuscades for the enemy. All houses, gardens, enclosures, &c. must be closely searched by the skirmishers, and no height, or village, from whence the neighbouring ground can be seen, must be left unexamined by them. It is hardly necessary to observe, that the arms of skirmishers should always be in the best order, and ready for immediate use.

Duties of skirmishers.

§ 5.

§ 5.

When an advanced guard approaches a village;

If a village should happen to lie on the road through which a column must unavoidably pass, it will first be examined by the advanced guard, after the manner that has been prescribed for patroles on similar occasions, and a report made to the commanding officer of the column. The commander of an advanced guard or flank patrole, will at all times make an exact report to the commanding officer of the column, of any thing extraordinary that may occur during the march, or of any remarkable feature of the country.

§ 6.

or is to pass a defilé;

An advanced guard, or flank patrole, will on no account enter a wood or defié, until a small party has previously passed through it, and closely examined it. In reconnoitring a wood, an advanced guard will follow the same directions as have been given for patroles, so that when the column arrives at the defilé, or wood, it may pass without risk or loss of time.

§ 7.

§ 7.

If the commander of the head of an advanced guard should have intelligence of the approach of an enemy's patrole, he will first halt, endeavour to discover the strength of it, and then fall back on the main body; the commanding officer of which, if the enemy is not in too great force, should try to conceal his men, suffer the enemy to approach, and endeavour to entangle him between his parties and the head of the column, when he may attack him without risk. If an advanced guard is set upon unawares by a body of the enemy in ambuscade, the officer commanding it must immediately attack; but it will depend upon what may be the general object of the move, whether he is to engage with his whole force, trusting to the column for support, or whether he is merely to keep the enemy in check, so as to gain the time sufficient for the column to make such dispositions as may be thought necessary. It is a maxim, however, and one which cannot be too strongly impressed upon the mind of every officer commanding an advanced guard, or flank patrole, that in the event of his being pursued by a considerable body of the enemy, he is by no means to fall back immediately upon the column: officers should therefore take precautions against any unforeseen accidents that may occur during the march, and attentively observe the ground by which a retreat may

or meets an enemy.

be

be effected. The commanding officer of an advanced guard is not to confine himself to the main body, but occasionally to visit the advanced and flank patroles, that he may make his own observasions, and trust as little as possible to the reports of others.

§ 8.

If an advanced guard meets an enemy in the night.

IF the advanced guard should meet the enemy in the night, the officer commanding it will immediately attack, if not with the whole, at least with part of his force, and not give the enemy time to force him back upon the column; he must exert himself to prevent confusion among his own men, but endeavour to spread dismay in the detachment of the enemy. A resolute officer, with a few determined men, may at night render the most important services; for even should he not be able to gain any solid advantage, still a spirited and well-timed attack will at least have the effect of embarrassing the enemy, during which time the column may form and prepare to act as the occasion may require. It is always useful, in these rencontres, to make prisoners, in order to find out the strength of the enemy, and what may have been the object of his march.

§ 9.

§ 9.

It is a rule that flank patroles are never to leave impracticable ground, or other obstacles, between them and the column; for example, if in the course of a march they meet with a morass, or piece of water of considerable extent, close to which the line of march is to pass; it would be a great fault to leave such an obstacle between the patrole and column, as it would be exposing the former to be cut off in sight of the column, by a detachment of the enemy, without the possibility of receiving succour. When a flank patrole therefore meets with any impediment of this sort, it will draw as near to the column as the local circumstance requires, and continue to march in this manner, until the nature of the ground suffers it to resume its usual station; for as long as a column is passing by a morass or lake it is sufficiently covered by them: the above rule is equally to be observed by all skirmishers from the flank patroles; but if a flank patrole should meet with a thicket or small wood, the skirmishers will immediately enter and examine it, and a small detachment should be sent round it, in order to prevent any concealed party of the enemy falling upon the rear of the column, after it has passed the wood.

When a flank patrole meets with any unpassable obstacle on the march.

§ 10.

§ 10.

When the column halts. If in the course of a march the column should halt, the advanced guard will of course do the same; the ank patroles and skirmishers making front outwards; and it is to be observed, that no defilé within a short distance of the advanced guard or flank patroles should be left unoccupied. The advanced guard should endeavour even to make itself master of the ground beyond the defilé, if it is only by sending a few men to take post there, that the column may be in security during the halt, and the men be suffered to rest themselves. Besides, by this precaution, the advanced guard will secure the pass of the defilé. It will of course be understood, that when a column halts, the advanced guard and flank patroles will post their own sentries, and thus form the pickets and chains of sentries for the whole column.

§ 11.

Of the rear guard. No column is ever to march without a rear guard, the strength of which must depend upon circumstances. The disposition of it is the same as the advanced guard, with this difference only, that the main body precedes the smaller. In marches where the

the enemy is supposed to be in front, the rear guard should be composed of a few trusty men, whose business it is to collect all stragglers, and to take up deserters.

§ 12.

A REAR guard is as much as possible to avoid en- *General directions for the conduct of a rear guard.* gaging the enemy, inasmuch as nothing more is usually expected from the officer commanding it, than to join the army without loss. He must, however, endeavour to execute his instructions, which generally have for their object to prevent the loss of baggage and capture of stragglers, and to keep the enemy at a distance from the column. The means of performing this service must depend upon the nature of the ground, and the relative situations of the column and the enemy. This, however, may be considered as a fixed principle, that the rear guard should dispute every defilé, as long as possible, in order to enable the column to gain ground: as soon as this object is attained, or the rear guard is obliged to leave the defilé, the next defilé must be gained as expeditiously as possible.

The officer commanding a rear guard is as much as possible to avoid passing a defilé in the presence

of

of a superior enemy; to this end he must, without loss of time, occupy the defilé, the moment the column has passed, without giving the enemy time to bring up more troops.

§ 13.

Of the conduct of rear guards of different columns relative to each other. When an army retires before an enemy in several columns, each having his own rear guard, they will preserve a communication with one another, and in common cover the retreat of the army. Suppose, for instance, an army retiring in three columns, and each having a defilé to pass, but the first having a better and shorter road outmarches the second; in this case the officer commanding the rear guard of the first must not give up the defilé, till he has ascertained that the rear guard of the second column is actually passing: the second is to observe the same conduct with regard to the third, and *vice versa*. For want of this precaution, a body of the enemy which had followed the first column, might attack the rear guard of the second in flank, which, as long as the rear guard of the first remains posted before the defilé, he cannot venture to do without risking himself to be taken in flank. This is an instance which affords to an officer the opportunity

of

of displaying his judgment of ground. Before an officer commanding a rear guard arrives at a defilé or village, which he must of necessity pass, if time permits him, he should send forward some intelligent men, to patrole to the right and left, and to discover the different passes, which he should occupy to guard against being cut off, and to effect his passage with the greater facility.

§ 14.

If a rear guard should be pursued by the enemy, it will divide itself into two bodies, which will continue to retreat in communication with one another, sending out several skirmishers, who will extend themselves by twos, and fire in retiring. The skirmishers must preserve as good a line as possible; the two bodies will retire alternately, the one covering the retreat of the other. If the enemy should press forward, the skirmishers will throw themselves on each flank, and endeavour by their fire to disconcert his attack. An enemy may sometimes be led to commit himself by a feigned retreat, and by leaving part of the corps in ambush, which may fall upon him with advantage, while in the heat of his pursuit. The officer commanding the skirmishers

Of the rear guard when pursued by the enemy.

must take care that in advancing and retreating, they do not extend themselves too much, and that the strictest attention is paid to his signals

§ 15.

Of the skirmishers of rear guards
OFFICERS of rear guards and flank patroles must be very careful to prevent their skimirshers loitering in any village: soldiers offending in this respect should be severely punished.

CHAP.

CHAP. III.

Of Pickets.

§ 1.

THE strength of the pickets must in a great measure depend on the ground it is intended they should occupy, the distance or proximity of the enemy, and the importance that may be attached to the post to which they are intended to give security. *Of posting pickets.*

Before the pickets are posted, as exact a knowledge as possible should be acquired of the country, in which particular care should be taken to ascertain all the approaches from defilés, villages, or from woods. No picket should be posted so as to be seen from a distance by the enemy, but behind a small wood or elevated ground, or hedge, or in a hollow: and it is well posted, provided its operations are not impeded by any of the above objects. The number of sentries required should in general regulate the force of pickets, which should be calculated to furnish three reliefs; but when the enemy is near at hand, it is usual to reinforce them, either that more sentries may be posted, or, that in case of attack they may be able to make a greater resistance.

§ 2

§ 2.

Of posting the sentries of pickets.

As soon as the picket arrives on the ground it is to occupy, the sentries must be posted; in doing which the officer should see that trusty men be fixed upon for the most important posts. On all advanced pickets the sentries must be doubled. The picket itself should be told off in two or four divisions, according to the strength of it: and to each a steady serjeant or corporal should be allotted. The general officer of the day usually fixes upon the spot for the picket, and the out-sentries. Particular circumstances may however render it necessary for the officer commanding it to make other arrangements afterwards; or he may put on more sentries at night, should he not think his post secure; but he must report what he has done to the general of the day.

§ 3.

Of reconnoitring.

When the sentries are posted, the commanding officer of a picket should next make it his business to inform himself of the nature of the country in his front: for this purpose he should endeavour to get from the village nearest him an intelligent man,

well

well acquainted with the country, with whom he should visit the environs, within a certain distance of his post, informing himself of the names of the places, rivulets, &c. and ascertaining the distance of the woods, villages, or defilés, still further in front. An officer should be particularly attentive to these points, as it will be expected, when the general or field officer visits his picket, that he will make a very exact report.

The officer relieving a picket should be made acquainted with every circumstance respecting the post by the officer coming off duty, who will explain to him the nature of the environs, and inform him of any occurrence that has happened. The former should not, however, solely rely on this information, but should make further enquiries, and endeavour to make himself still more perfect in his knowledge of the post, ground, &c.

§ 4.

SENTRIES should be so posted as to secure one another from being cut off, and most advantageously for discovering the approach of the enemy. No sentry, however, should be posted, on any account, at a greater distance from the picket, than that

Of the distance sentries should be posted from the picket, that at which a musket shot may easily be heard, under any circumstance of wind, weather, or local situation. If sentries should be posted so far from one another, that an enemy might, during the night, pass unperceived between them, it will be necessary that one of them should constantly patrole to the next sentry, the other remaining fixed on his post. On advanced pickets, sentries should be relieved every hour, between which it will be the officer's duty to see that this order, respecting patroles, is strictly complied with.

---

§ 5.

O. posting them by night.

THE situation of a picket frequently requires that the sentries should not occupy the same post by night as by day, and particularly when the out-posts of the two armies are so near that the sentries are within sight of each other, which might induce an enterprising enemy, from his frequent opportunity of observing their situation, to attempt carrying them off in the night; the officer will therefore fix upon proper points to which he may withdraw his sentries, and thereby avoid this risk. If this precaution had not already been directed by the general officer f the day, a report should be immediately made to

him

him of it; excepting in this instance, no officer commanding a picket is to make any change in the disposition of his sentries, unless, for the greater security of his post, he should think it necessary to augment the number of them.

In the day time sentries should be posted on the most elevated ground, the better to discover the neighbouring country; but at night they should retire so as to have the high ground before them, as an object is far more easily discerned at night from below, than in looking down from an hill. In situations where pickets or advanced posts are at a considerable distance from each other, and not separated by morasses, lakes, or other impassable obstacles, but where the country between is interspersed with thickets or enclosures, it is necessary at night to place single or even double sentries on the flanks, and towards the rear, to prevent the enemy from stealing in between, and falling on your posts from behind. This precaution is principally necessary in dark and stormy nights.

When pickets are near each other, the ground on which they are posted should be taken up in such a manner, that should the enemy venture to attack any one of them, he may not be able to effect it without exposing his flank.

§ 6.

Particular instructions for sentries.

SENTRIES are never unnecessarily to expose their arms, particularly when the sun shines, as the glittering of them may be seen at a great distance; they must also be forbid, under pain of severe punishment, to strike fire, or smoke tobacco in the night: nor are they on any account to be permitted, during cold or rainy weather, to wear caps which cover the ears, as they must necessarily prevent them from hearing, and in such weather, above all, the utmost vigilance is required. The sentries, who are invariably to be doubled, will face outwards towards the enemy; one observing the country, bye roads, &c. to the right, the other to the left.

§ 7.

When any person approaches their post.

WHEN a sentry hears or sees any person approach him by night, he must challenge loud—*Who's there?* and immediately advance a few paces, with his arms cocked and ported; then calls—*Halt!—Countersign?* Even if the countersign is right, the person is not to be permitted to pass, till the sentry is convinced that he is not an enemy; but should there be any thing in his appearance or language to create suspicion

suspicion, or that he is not perfectly still, when he is ordered to halt, the sentry must fire. When a sentry is posted, the objects of his particular attention must be pointed out to him; besides which he is to watch the sentries on his right and left, and should either of them disappear, he is immediately to report it to the serjeant or officer of the picket. No stranger is to be suffered to approach within eight or ten paces of him, nor is he to hold any communication with any one whetever, while he is on his post.

§ 8.

On the approach of a flag of truce, one sentry will advance in order to oblige it to halt at some distance from his post; the other go back to the picket to report the circumstance. The officer or non-commissioned officer should then repair to the spot, order the persons composing the flag of truce to be blindfolded, and take them back with him to the picket; or if there should be an house near at hand, he should order them to be conducted thither under an escort, which will remain with them. The officer will then take what letters the flag may have brought, for which he will give a receipt, and send them immediately to head-quarters. The further disposal

On the arrival of an officer or flag of truce from the enemy

of the flag of truce will depend on the orders sent from head-quarters; but as long as the flag is detained at the outposts, no one is on any account to be permitted to hold any conversation with the persons composing it; in every other respect they are to be treated with becoming civility.

---

§ 9.

or of deserters or travellers; No deserters, especially if they are mounted, must be allowed to come near a sentry, particularly by night, but must be made to halt at a distance: the sentry then sends to the picket for a non-commissioned officer and some men, who will disarm and conduct them to the officer. If there should be more than one deserter, the non-commissioned officer must let them approach him only one by one. At night, deserters must have sentries placed over them, and be kept at a small distance from the picket till day-light, when they will be sent by the first opportunity to some post in the rear, and from thence be forwarded to head-quarters. Officers at the advanced posts are on no account to detain a deserter of our own army, who may be apprehended, or may be returning from the enemy, for the purpose of sending him straight to his regiment;
but

but immediately on the apprehension of any such must order them to be conducted to head-quarters. Peasants, or travellers, arriving at an advanced sentry, whether from the front or rear, will be stopped and sent to the picket to be examined, and should there be any reason to suspect them, they must be detained, and a report made to head-quarters.

§ 10.

STILL less are sentries to suffer any number of men, exceeding two or three, whether soldiers or peasants, who come from the front, to approach too near their post. In the day-time one sentry will advance, halt them, and try to discover what they are. If it should be a detachment of soldiers, he will conduct the commander of it, or if a number of peasants, he will take one of them to the officer commanding the picket, who will either suffer them to pass, or go himself with a party from his post to examine them more closely, as circumstances may require. At night this precaution is still more necessary: if then any body of men, though announcing themselves as a detachment of the army, and even in possession of the countersign, should arrive at the advanced sentries, they must order them to halt, and report their arrival

or when any body of men approach their post.

arrival to the picket, the officer of which will send a non-commissioned officer with a party to examine them. On this occasion an officer is not to trust to the uniform, or even to the *watch-word* being right; but is to inform himself of the cause of their arrival at his post, and of every circumstance that may lead to an explanation. He must further demand the pass or written order: if this is found to be correct, and the officer is satisfied in every respect that there is no risk, the detachment may be suffered to pass his picket, which, on the first arrival of the detachment at his post, will have been ordered under arms.

Such precautions should never be omitted, as there are numberless instances of posts having been carried off by people in disguise, or parties of one army dressing themselves in the clothing of another. Sentries too should be cautioned not to let carts or waggons come too near them, nor pass without being previously examined, particularly those carrying hay, wood, or otherwise high loaded; as it is not uncommon for armed men to come concealed by such a conveyance, with a view to carry off the advanced sentries, or some small post.

§ 11.

ONE half of the picket at least must be constantly under arms during the night; these will be posted so far in front, as, in case of a sudden attack, to give time to the remainder to get under arms. The latter may be allowed to rest themselves, without, however, quitting their arms for an instant. An alarm post will be assigned them, where they will instantly form on the picket's being attacked, in order that when the advanced part has given its fire and retreated, this may also fire with effect. At night, and in cold weather, when there are fires at the pickets, they should be made in the rear, be as much concealed as possible, and the men be suffered to warm themselves by turns, and not more than two or three at a time.

Of the duty of pickets by night.

It sometimes happens that the advanced posts and pickets of an army must be placed in extremely exposed situations, and that the patroles cannot be sent sufficiently forward to get intelligence of the enemy; the general or field officer of the day will then signify whether any, and which of the pickets should remain under arms all night; in this case no man, except upon the most urgent necessity, is to quit his post.

§ 12.

Of detached pickets. A PICKET would derive great security, and avoid being easily surprised, by detaching at night small parties from two to three hundred paces to the right and left, which, in case of attack of the main body, would be most advantageously posted for its protection, and for galling the enemy by their fire on his flanks. Pickets, as well as advanced sentries, should remove at night from the spot they occupy during the day; so that if the enemy, from the observations he may have made of the post, should attempt to surprise it, he may himself be led into an error. In cold weather, when fires are requisite, it is adviseable that the position of the picket be frequently changed, and the fires left burning. If the enemy means to attack, he naturally directs his march on the fires, and when he arrives there, finding the post abandoned, he may reasonably suppose the picket has retired: should he loiter on the spot, or be at all off his guard, he may himself be attacked with every advantage.

§ 13.

THE non-commissioned officer commanding a detached picket or other small post during the night, as well as the advanced sentries, must be instructed, that in case of attack by surprise, and being forced to fall back, they are not to retire upon the main body, but to the spot which the picket occupied in the day-time, and from thence continue their retreat on the flank of the picket, so that if the enemy should pursue, he must necessarily expose himself to be taken in flank. The officer commanding the picket will by this means have it at his option, to attack the enemy to a manifest advantage, or to effect his retreat unperceived.

When the detached posts of a picket are attacked.

---

§ 14.

As attacks of pickets, or advanced posts, by night, are generally made with a superior force, and seldom undertaken without a strong reserve, it will, in this instance, be the business of an officer commanding a picket, to give the alarm to the posts in his rear, rather than attempt to make a vigorous resistance. As soon, therefore, as he finds his post seriously

Of the duty of an officer commanding a picket, when attacked.

ously attacked, he must endeavour, with the chief of his force, to reach the nearest defilé, or *post of support*, leaving, however, skirmishers in his rear, and on his flanks, who must keep up a constant fire, the better to cover his retreat, and spread the alarm. An officer must, however, be very cautious not to abandon his post till he is certain of the superiority of the enemy. When a retreat cannot be made in good order, from the suddenness of the enemy's attack, and superiority of his force, for the purpose of gaining time an officer may resolve upon a desperate and vigorous attack, with whatever he can collect of his picket: the enemy will probably at first give way; but the officer of the picket is on no account to pursue, his own object being only to effect a retreat, and to reach with the greatest expedition the first post where he can make a stand.

If the picket should be attacked in the day-time, the officer will take his measures according to the strength of the enemy. If weak, he will form an ambuscade, and endeavour to cut him off; if in force, he must with part of his men form a reserve, and with the remainder in separate bodies retire alternately: he may try to check the pursuit, by letting the enemy discover the reserve; but should he be closely pressed, before he can receive support from some post in his rear, he must endeavour, by means of the small detached bodies of his picket, to annoy the enemy in flank.

§ 18.

§ 15.

When a sentry is posted, the countersign only is to be given to him; but the non-commissioned officer of a picket or patrole will receive the *watch-word;* without which no patrole should be allowed to pass, and which should always be given in a low voice, by the serjeant of the patrole to him of the picket. The field officer commanding the pickets may, if circumstances should require it, change the countersign in the course of the night; but the watch-word need never be changed, except in the instance of a non-commissioned officer deserting. In case of the countersign being changed, the neighbouring advanced posts must immediately be informed of it, to prevent mistakes and false alarms.

Of the watch-word and countersign.

§ 16.

When any authentic intelligence is received of the enemy, the officer of the picket is immediately to make a written report of it to head-quarters, and to the commanding officers of such regiments as are near him. These reports must be made with the greatest accuracy; and it is one of the principal duties of an officer on a picket, when near the enemy,

Of reports.

my, to get every intelligence of and report his movements. A written report should be made every evening, and sent by a non-commissioned officer to the field officer of the day.

―――――

§ 17.

Particular duties of an officer on picket. On picket and other duties, where the service is inseparable from the greatest hardships, it is the duty of every officer to set his men a good example, not to be lying down or resting himself when the men are under arms, nor to go under cover while they are without shelter, but share, in common with them, every danger and fatigue: by his example, soldiers will submit cheerfully, and without murmuring, to any inconvenience; it is also the best means of securing their attention and confidence.

In the day-time, if it can be done without risk, he will suffer the men to rest themselves, but he himself must frequently visit the sentries, give them the necessary instructions, and inform himself of the exact situation of his own post, and of those near him. He should attentively observe the nature of the ground, so as in any event to take advantage of it.

CHAP.

CHAP. IV.

Of Patroles from the Pickets.

§ 1.

With a view to ensure the tranquillity and security of the camp, the ground in front of the pickets should be constantly patroled day and night.

General rule.

---

§ 2.

It may frequently happen, and particularly in bad weather, or when the wind blows strong towards the enemy, that the small patroles in front of the camp may be carried off by the enemy unperceived by the pickets; to guard against which, parties of two or three men must be sent from the pickets, whose business it will be to advance so far in front of the chain of sentries, as to be able to observe the movements of the patroles.

Of patroles from pickets.

§ 3.

Additional patroles by night. SMALL patroles must in addition, be sent out from the pickets, particularly during the night: some to visit the roads by which an enemy might approach with a view of penetrating between the posts; others to visit the chain of sentries, and see that they are watchful. If the country in front of the pickets is enclosed, the morning patroles should closely examine the roads leading through it, that the enemy, who may have concealed himself during the night, may not surprise the picket, or be permitted to reconnoitre the position.

4.

Of visiting patroles. PATROLES which are to visit the sentries, should consist of a non-commissioned officer and four men. The non-commissioned officer puts himself at their head; the men following at the distance of thirty or forty paces, in order to be ready to support him, in case of necessity. When the patrole approaches a sentry, the latter challenges him; and, on the former answering *Patrole*, the countersign will be demanded. No person should, however, be allowed

to

to approach nearer to a sentry than eight or ten paces. The countersign should not be given louder than is absolutely necessary for the sentry to hear it, for fear of any enemy, or spy, who may have concealed himself near his post.

§ 5.

The patroles which are employed immediately in front of the pickets, need not consist of more than a non-commissioned officer and four men; of these one man moves on fifty paces in front; the non-commissioned officer and two men following, and examining, as they go along, the ground on each side of the road; the fourth man keeps at a little distance in the rear, that he may be able to give timely notice to his comrades, in case the enemy should have passed unperceived, and be lying any where in ambush. In hazy weather they must keep closer to each other. Where the ground is much intersected, they should not advance above two hundred paces in front of the sentries; but where it is open, the distance may be increased. In the course of the day, the officer of the picket will be able to point out, pretty nearly, the ground that is to be patroled at night: and that the space between the pickets

Patroles to the front of the chain of sentries.

may be constantly visited, all patroles of this sort will proceed so far to the right and left as to pass the first sentry of the neighbouring picket.

When two patroles meet in the night, the non-commissioned officer of that which challenges first, is to receive the *watch-word*. When the answer *(patrole)* is given to the challenge, the advanced man charges his bayonet, and calls out, *Stand Patrole*. The non-commissioned officer of the first then advances, and receives the watchword, and if that should be right, he gives the countersign, that each may be satisfied of the other being a friend. If the patrole meets with the enemy, the first object is to give an alarm to the picket.

§ 6.

Of patroles with the relieved sentries. At day-break patroles may be made with the sentries just relieved, who are then formed in two divisions. With one, a non-commissioned officer, immediately after the relief, patroles to the front, in order that if the enemy should have formed an ambuscade during the night, it may be discovered. With the other, for further security, the line of sentries will be again visited.

§ 7.

§ 7.

PATROLES for this service should consist of from twelve to sixteen men, and will in general march at day-break, in order to reconnoitre the villages, woods, &c. in the neighbourhood. They are more particularly to examine the places from which an attack may be expected, to get intelligence of the enemy, and to push on as far as they can without exposing themselves to the risk of being cut off. Nothing is so disgraceful to an officer on an advanced picket as allowing himself to be surprised, to avoid which he should examine in person, the ground in his front and on his flanks, particularly such parts as may offer shelter for an ambuscade. By a strict observance of these principles he will generally defeat the projects of the enemy. *Of patroles for the purpose of reconnoitring.*

FINIS.

Printed and bound by Antony Rowe Ltd, Eastbourne

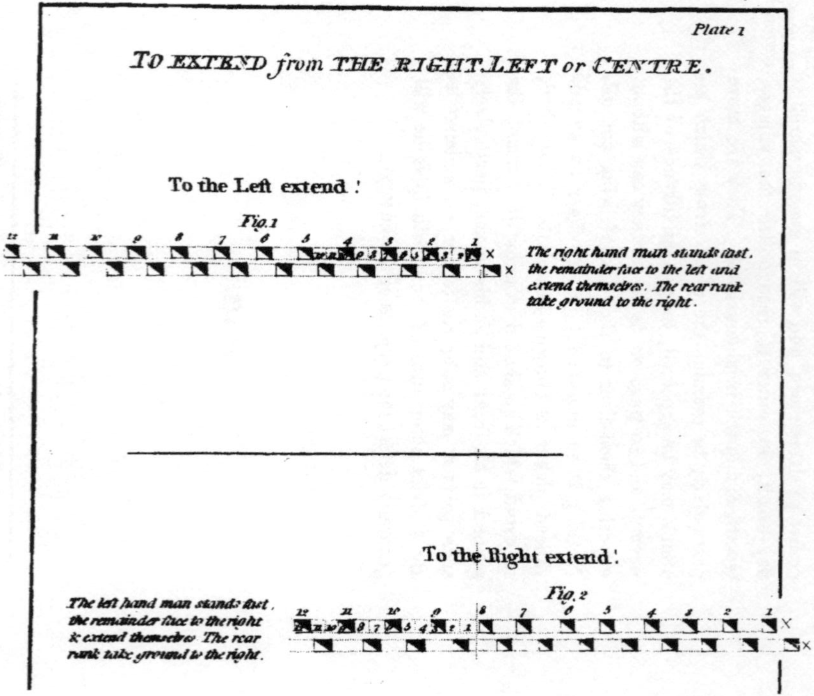

Plate 1

TO EXTEND from THE RIGHT, LEFT or CENTRE.

To the Left extend:

Fig. 1

The left hand man stands fast, the remainder face to the right & extend themselves. The rear rank take ground to the right.

The right hand man stands fast, the remainder face to the left and extend themselves. The rear rank take ground to the right.

To the Right extend:

Fig. 2

From the Centre extend!

Fig. 3

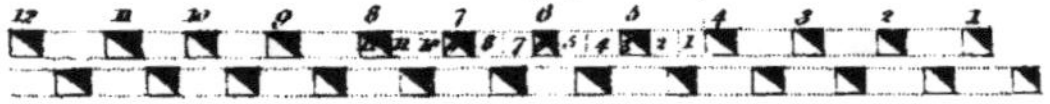

The center file stands fast the remainder face outwards & extend themselves.

Plate 2

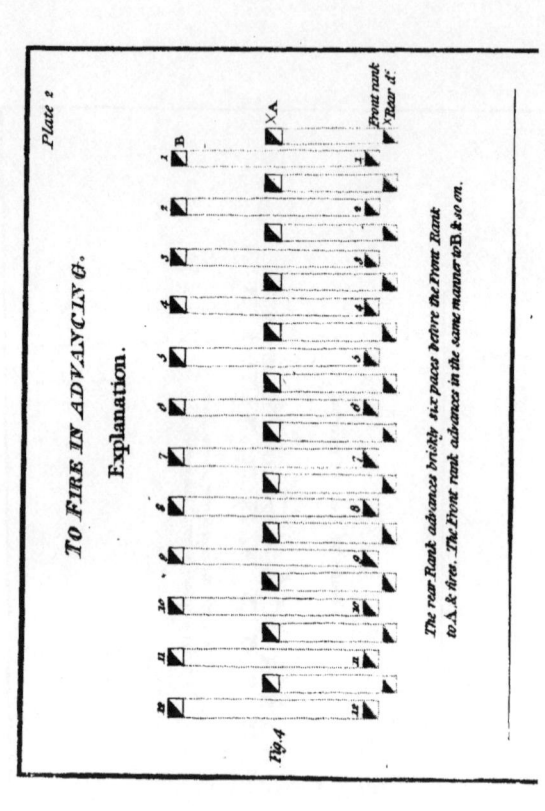

TO FIRE IN ADVANCING.
Explanation.

The rear Rank advances briskly six paces before the Front Rank to A. & fire. The Front rank advances in the same manner to B. & so on.

Fig. 4

TO FIRE IN RETREATING.

Explanation.

The front rank having given one fire, faces to the right about & marches 12 Paces to A. The rear rank then gives its fire & retreats 12 Paces behind the front rank to B, & so on.

Fig. 3

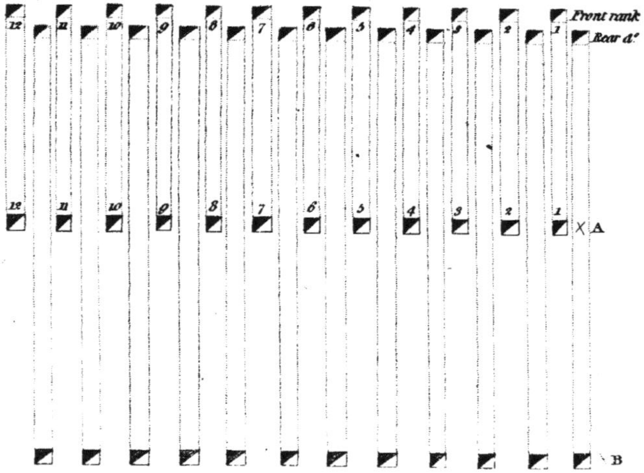

Plate 3

OF SKIRMISHING.

Explanation.

3 will march 50 Paces to A
4 .... no .... B and
Extend themselves to the Right
till C is in a Line with D.

Fig. 6

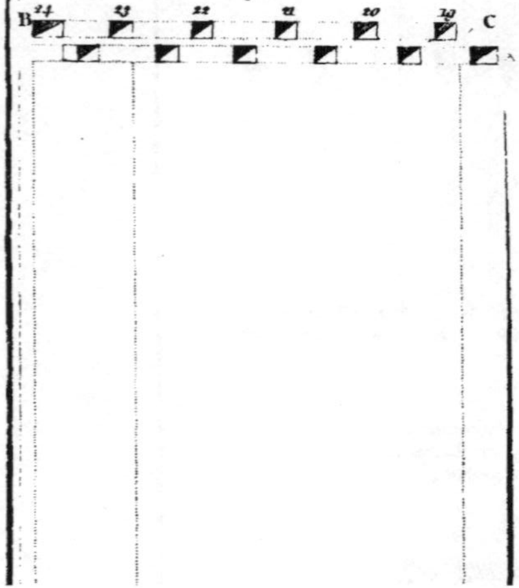

2 Will march 50 Paces to A
1 .... no .... B
Extend themselves to the Left
till C is in a Line with D.

Fig. 7

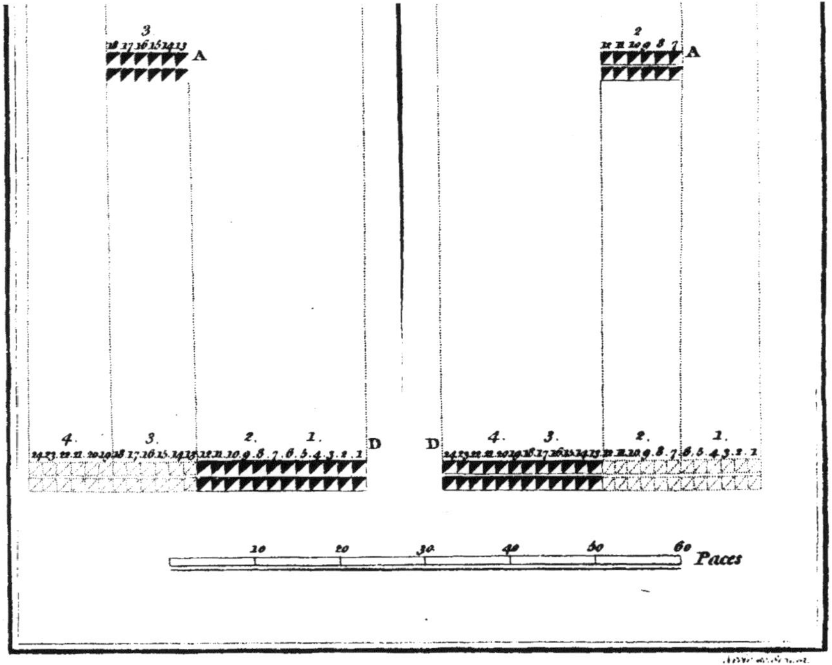
A
A
D
D
10
20
30
40
50
60
Paces

Plate 4

The Company retreating in close order across a Plain.

Fig. 8

Explanation.

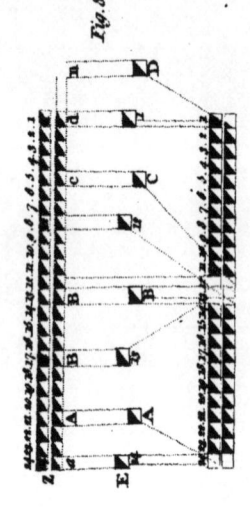

1.2.3...24 ABCD are the left & right Files of the Platoons which were in VXYZ. E shew their Position 13 Paces in the rear for the purpose of covering the retreat of the Company which when arrived at E fronts on account of being attacked by the Enemys Cavalry, and when the retreat is sounded the Files fall into their proper Intervals.

Formation of the Chain.

Explanation.

The 4th Section remains behind as a Reserve. The rest advance 30 Paces and extend themselves to the left in Divisions of two Files each, with Intervals of ten Paces between them.

Fig. 9

Plate 5

FORMATION OF THE CHAIN.

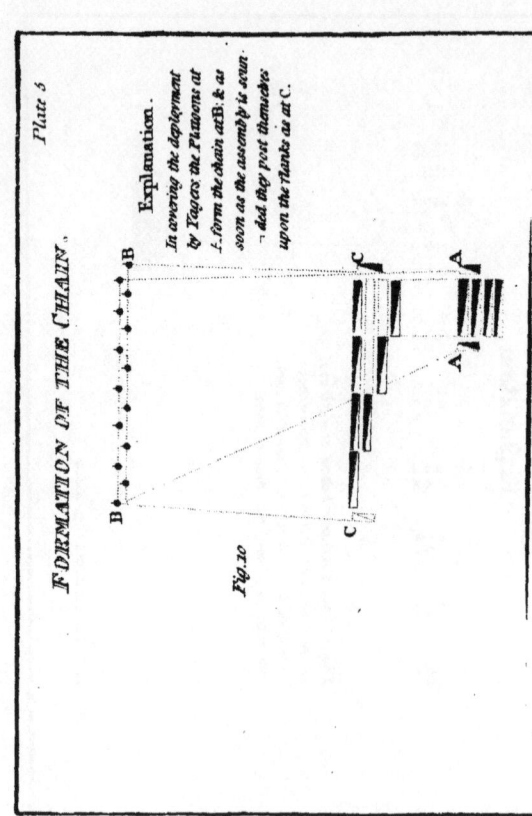

Fig. 10

Explanation.
In covering the deployment by Jagers the Platoons at 1. form the chain at B: & as soon as the assembly is sounded they post themselves upon the flanks as at C.

The Formation and Disposition of a Company of Riflemen or Light Infantry which is to form an advanced Guard

Fig. 11

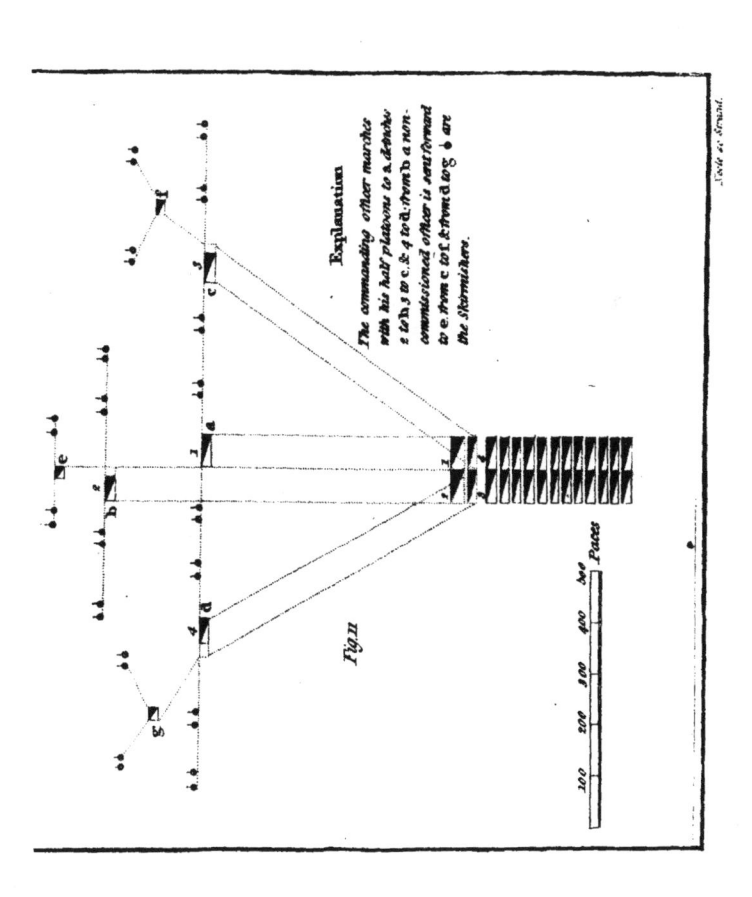

Explanation

The commanding officer marches with his half platoons to a, denotes 2 to b, 3 to c, & 4 to d: from b a non-commissioned officer is sent forward to e, from c to f, & from d to g: are the Skirmishers.

Plate 8

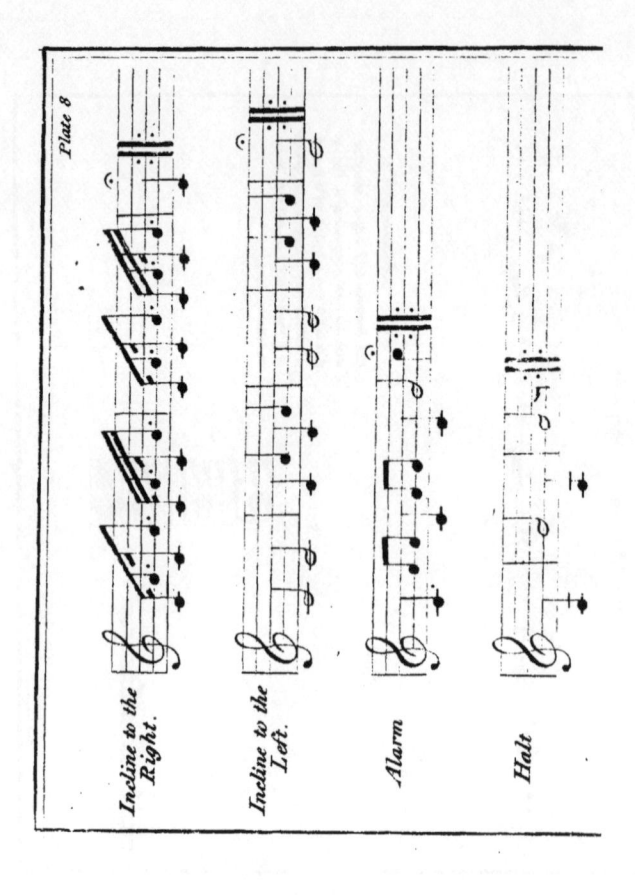

Incline to the Right.

Incline to the Left.

Alarm

Halt

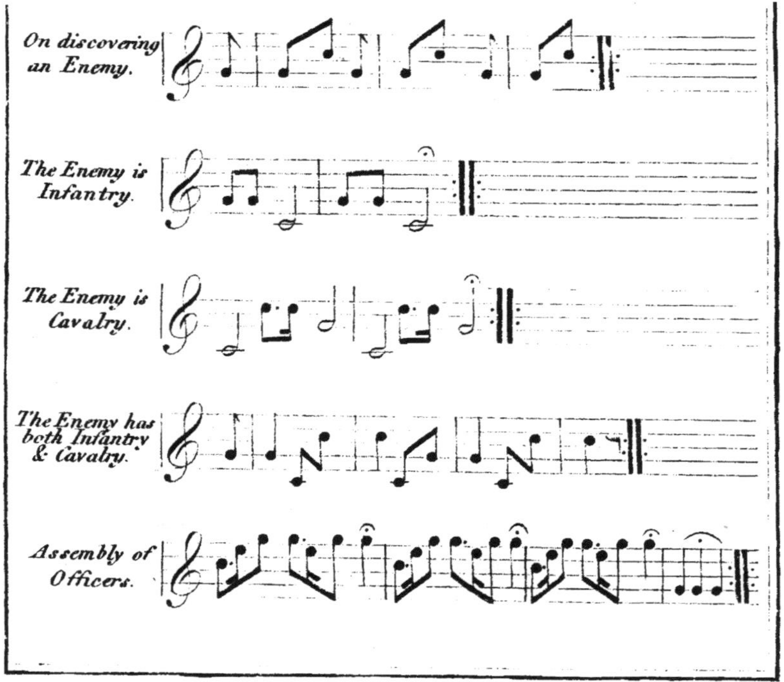
On discovering an Enemy.
The Enemy is Infantry.
The Enemy is Cavalry.
The Enemy has both Infantry & Cavalry.
Assembly of Officers.

Signals of the Bugle Horn,
in the
Movements of Light Troops.

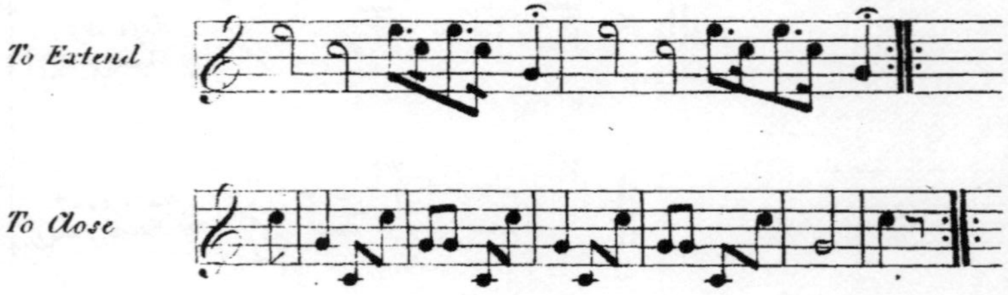

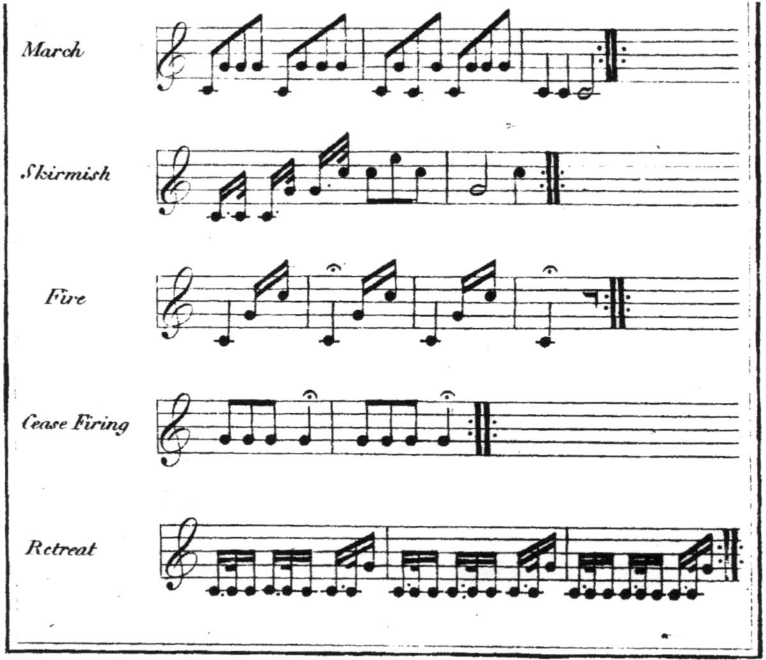
March
Skirmish
Fire
Cease Firing
Retreat

Plate 6

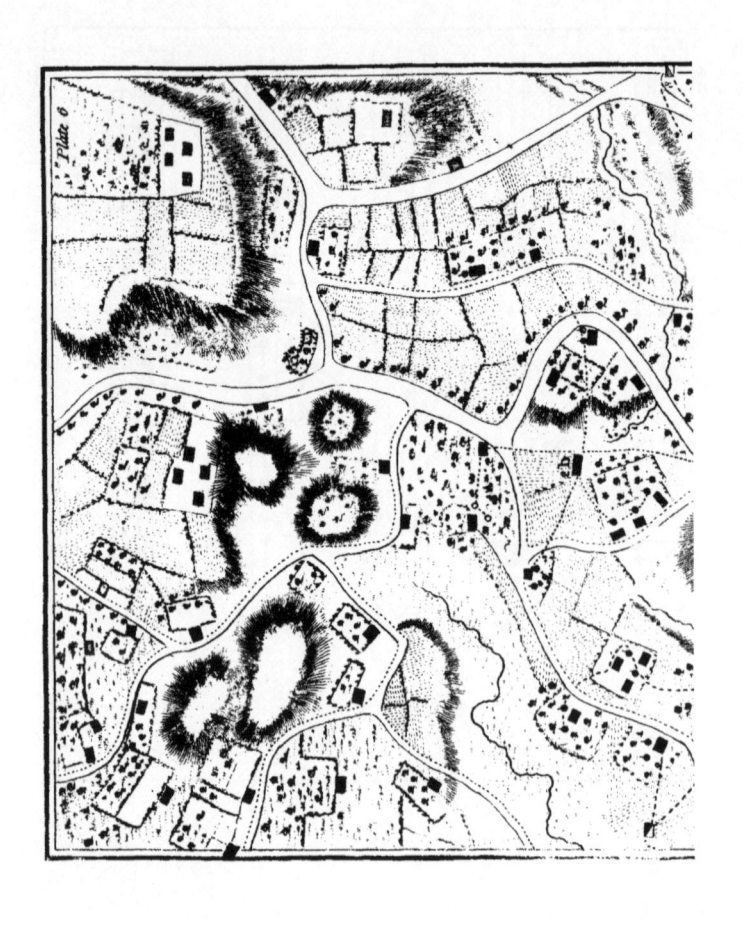

Fig. II

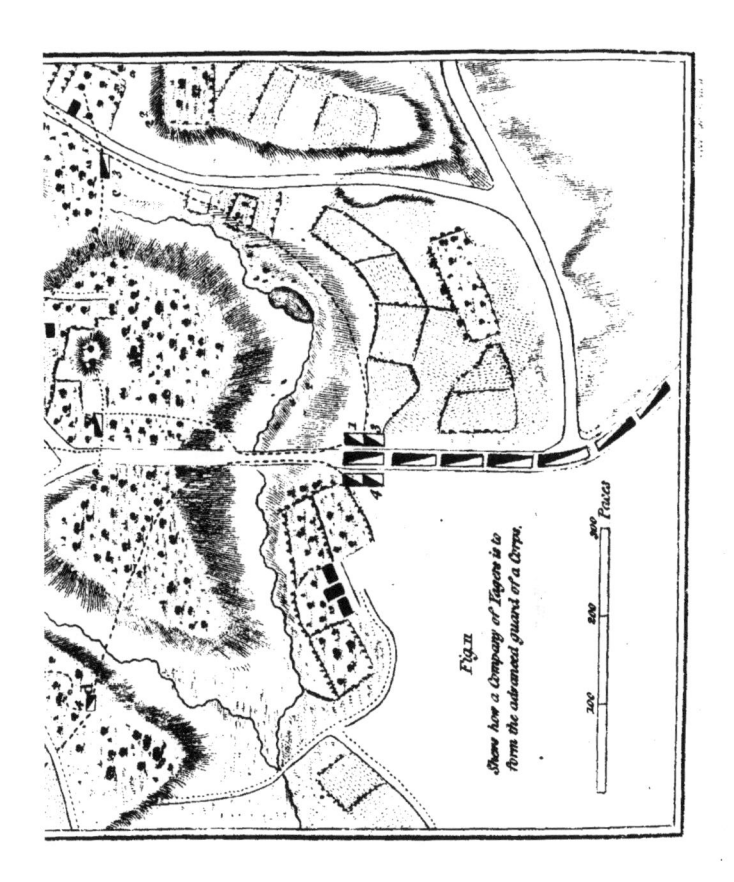

Shews how a Company of Yägers is to form the advanced guard of a Corps.

Printed in Great Britain
by Amazon.co.uk, Ltd.,
Marston Gate.